What Goes Unsaid

Laiba Ali

BookLeaf Publishing

India | USA | UK

Made with ❤ on the BookLeaf Publishing Platform
www.bookleafpub.in
www.bookleafpub.com

Dedication

To the people who find solace in the cold hands of
poetry,
to the people who are mute at the mercy of emotions,
to the people, in some way, just like me.

Preface

This has been a wild ride! I remember, just three weeks ago, sitting in my freezing cold classroom when my teacher told us about this challenge: write a piece of fiction or poetry every day for twenty-one days, and at the end, submit it for publication. I was thrilled. Finally, I had a chance to turn my lifelong hobby—the very pillar of my personality—into something others could read and (hopefully) be inspired by. That feeling alone was enough to warm me up.

But let me tell you, it hasn't been easy. Writer's block hits you like that gut-wrenching moment right before you throw up. You know it's coming, but you're too prideful to admit it. Then the signs start—your mouth waters, your stomach churns—and you're just like, "Yup, here we go." That's how I felt throughout this challenge. The ideas were stubborn, and putting them into words? Even more so.

Yet, here I am, presenting to you what feels like a puddle of my emotions, thoughts, and words. Yes, it's messy, like a puddle of vomit. But it's real. Each piece in this book reflects a part of me I'm still discovering. My hope is that you find pieces of yourself within these pages too.

The freezing cold letters on my laptop that worked tirelessly to bring my thoughts to life, I hope you enjoy the result.
And hey, sorry if I just ruined your appetite. I lost mine too.

Acknowledgements

First off, I'd like to appreciate the chicken curry my mom made—it's absolutely delicious.
Speaking of parents, thank you to my mom and dad for believing in me even when I didn't believe in myself.
To my friends, thank you for bringing joy and laughter into my everyday routine.
To my teachers, for guiding me and introducing me to this unique opportunity.
To the incredible publishers at BookLeaf, who work tirelessly to turn dreams into reality.
And finally, thank you to *me*. I stayed up late when I didn't want to, stepped out of my comfort zone, and poured my heart and soul into every word of this book.
Thank you, everyone!

1. . What is Wrong With Me?

I eat and I eat,
yet I am never satisfied.

A monster overlooks the mirror,
begging me to kill it.

I stab it every night,
with a weapon that spares no one.

Every night I stab,
and everyday, it's back.

2. . I Gaze Upon Her

I gaze upon her,
her smile shines
like an angel's wings
upon the earth.
she is my heaven.

I gaze upon her,
her eyes cold and piercing
like the devil's,
when he guides you to sin.
she is my hell.

I gaze upon her,
her gait ethereal
like a fairy hopping about.
she is my life.

I gaze upon her,
her lifeless body
buried among many.
she is my death.

3.. Womb and Soil

The mother looks upon her child,
with a love borne only in the womb.

The child looks upon his mother,
with a glance borne only from innocence.

If the love of a child is permanent;
If the love of a child is immortal,

Then tell me why,

The mother looks upon his grave,
with a love borne not only in the womb,
but also in the soil.

4. . The River

The river does not flow in daylight,
It is still, stagnant.
The river does not flow in daylight,
It cannot disclose its destination.

The river flows in the moonlight,
It is filled with the tears of man.
The river flows in the moonlight,
like a kiss between two lovers.

Her veins do not flow in daylight,
It is still with grief.
Her veins do not flow in daylight,
It cannot disclose its destination.

Her veins flow in the moonlight,
It is filled with tears of self.
Her veins flow in the moonlight,
like life flows into death with a kiss.

5. . Why not Love?

She writes of many things,
but not of love.

She writes of death, she writes of tragedy,
she writes of pain, she writes of misery.

She tells me, "What is the purpose of love,
if even the stars are to burn away?"

I wonder, who is this shadowed soul,
that turned her notebook from,

"Love is senseless, when the end is near,"
to "Even after the stars burn up, my dear,"

6.. The Plant of Love

There is a place somewhere,
that holds the plant of love.

They say it grows with the blood of lovers,
and withers with the blood of fools.

I went to that place, with a vile of my blood,
with a warm hand, I poured it into the soil.

I watched it grow, taller than the trees,
taller than the birds, taller than the clouds.

It reached the skies, stopped,
and withered away, near my cold hands.

7.. Rank 2

I saw her cries from afar,
looking at the paper on the board.

"Rank 2," she read, I'd never felt happier;
I found a victorious joy in her victorious grief.

If I was so happy,
If I was so content,

Why did my stomach clench, when
I saw the comforting hand on her shoulder,
telling her that he still loves her?

8.. You Can Be Sure

The dead man looks up from his grave,
as snowflakes fall in the fields of June.

When fire feels like ice,
and the birds yell curses in their melody,

The thunderstorms put you to ease,
rain showers feel like glass shards,

That is when you can be sure,
that you have fallen in love.

9.. What Will You Do for Fame?

"Do you want fame, young man?"
The voice asked.

"Yes, I want fame," I replied.
"Bring me three of your most hated articles, then,"
It announced.

And so, I brought it, the three articles.
One from my mother, one from my father,
and one from my lover.

Cameras flashed everywhere around me,
their lights are bright.
So why can I see only darkness?

The darkness in front, the darkness behind,
and the darkness beside.
"No, I don't want fame," I begged.

The darkness laughed.

10. . A Gloomy Day

I walked out of my house, a gloomy day,
An old man, with kids, glanced.

I walked into the shops, a gloomy day.
A young man, fit and proper, waved.

I walked back home, a gloomy day.
A man, similar to I, talked endlessly.

I opened my window, a gloomy day.
He, with his serious stare, devoid of expression,

Passed by my house, paying no attention to I,
A joyful day, for sure.

11. . The Painting

There is a painting, high up top.
Give it your prized possession,
and it will tell you your fate.

I gave it, an article of silver,
It said to me, "You will end horribly,"

I gave it, an article of gold,
It said to me, "You will live a life of luxury,"

I gave it, an article of my lover,
It said to me, "You are a fool,"

I have been wary of such artworks since,
those which tell me the truth.

12. . Discipline

It is more silent than a graveyard,
belongings arranged neatly.

The laughter of the room,
enclosed in history books.

The cheer of the room,
strangled in discipline.

A mysterious figure stands,
he talks of arcane things,

He shows peace, he shows war.
He shows protest, he shows life;
with his dead, dead voice.

The lifeless bodies listen,
a shell of what they once were.

13. . The Answers

I saw a woman looking out the window,
I wondered, what is she thinking about?

Are her thoughts woven in the same
complexity as mine are?

I saw a man walking down the street,
I wondered, where is he going?

Are his destinations,
as fruitful as mine?

I saw a child, dancing about happily,
I wondered, what is she so happy about?

Can her happiness,
be mine?

I saw an old man feeding the birds,
I wondered, what has caused him to live so long?

Is this, the peak of life?

I looked at myself, a mere quilt

of my many experiences.

I looked at the many people outside,
a mere quilt of their experiences,

And I found my answers.

14. . Past

Who knew an affair so brief,
could leave such a lasting void?

Those fleeting nights, spent in folly,
those long days, spent away from each other...

Hidden laughs, stolen glances,
in the middle of an unsuspecting crowd.

And then, you went away,
somewhere better for you,
someone better for you.

Though you may spend your days
cultivating a new life, a new happiness,
I still think about the one you left behind.

15.. My Notebook

I drown the voice of the teacher out,
looking into the pages of my notebook.

A small figure approaches them,
and tells me to flip the pages.

He slays the enemies, wins hearts,
he's a drop of rain in a drought.

He jumps over the equations,
brings me to a world of art.

Suddenly, he goes. He looks up,
and hides,

For the teacher stands near me,
looking into the pages of my notebook.

16.. Absent

I stare at the empty seat beside me,
among the many filled ones.

Laughs and giggles surround me,
in a circle full of life.

Radiant groups of friends,
their closeness apparent.

I cannot talk to them, the way I talk to her.
Once again, I yawn,

Staring at the empty side beside me.

17.. A Story in a Look

They say, the eyes are the window to the soul,
and my dear, this window has always been open.

You have heard the words I will never speak,
the expressions I will never make,
the ways in which I will never act.

You know the story of each freckle on my face,
each scar on my arm,
each birthmark on my body.

You were the food my famine needed,
the water my drought needed,
the life, my life needed.

You walk past me in the hallway, scoffing,
and the connection we built.

Yet, in each of your indifferent glances,
I can see a story as deep as mine.

18.. Fourteen

I am one among the pairs,
my other half.

Standing among the other pairs,
I anticipate her voice.

Her deep laughter, her familiar face,
I miss the ways we hid,

At the back of the class,
getting caught and separated.

Our adventures on the computers,
two screens, two thousand memories.

Maybe one day,
in another life,
in another universe,

We are fourteen again, sitting together,
making memories next to each other,
instead of miles and miles away.

19.. Her

The world is against me once again,
and I am left to face it alone.

I try to drown out the laughter,
no time for celebration now,

I write and write, about anything, really;
I do senseless things,
I think weird things.

My silence grows, with the noise around me.
My mind blanks, I don't know what to think,

And then, she calls.

20.. Drunk Words

Drunk words are sober thoughts, they say.
But I don't think so.

Drunk words are false thoughts,
because when you look at me;

I see rage in your eyes,
amongst a life of love.

I hear misery in your words,
amongst the many kind words you say.

I feel hatred, from your loving embrace.
And when you mutter, "I love you,"

With a bottle of wine,
all I hear is a phrase that could be.

www.ingramcontent.com/pod-product-compliance
Lightning Source LLC
LaVergne TN
LVHW021354200726
843509LV00014B/2852